The **Humanist Philosophers' Group** aims t( rational approach to public ethical issues. Th(discussions between the philosophers listed b members of the group:

David Archard, University of St Andrews
Julian Baggini, editor *The Philosophers' Magazine*
Piers Benn, Imperial College
Simon Blackburn, University of Cambridge
Peter Cave, The City University and The Open University
Michael Clark, University of Nottingham
Antony Duff, University of Stirling
Alan Haworth, University of North London
Brendan Larvor, University of Hertfordshire
Sandra Marshall, University of Stirling
Richard Norman, University of Kent
David Papineau, King's College, London
Jonathan Rée
Ben Rogers, Institute for Public Policy Research
Peter Simons, University of Leeds
Suzanne Uniacke, University of Hull
Nigel Warburton, The Open University
Stephen Wilkinson, University of Keele

Previous publications by the Humanist Philosophers' Group are *For your own good?* and *Religious schools: the case against*. Both are available from the British Humanist Association.

Humanist Philosophers' Group

What Is Humanism?

The problem of definition

The rejection of religion

Optimism about progress

Optimism about values

Which values?

Optimism in the face of human mortality

The problem of definition revisited

What Is Humanism?

The problem of definition

'What is humanism?' This looks like a fair question. Many people call themselves 'humanists', and use the word to refer to their most fundamental beliefs about the nature of the world and the meaning of human life. Other people may encounter the word 'humanist', think that it sounds attractive and may apply to them, but be unsure whether to describe themselves as humanists, and at that point they're likely to want to know more about what humanism is. How are they to be answered? There is no humanist Church and no humanist Creed, no Holy Book and no set of beliefs which all humanists have to accept. More worryingly, it is difficult to find a consensus. Ask people who call themselves 'humanists' what they mean by the word, and you're likely to get various different answers. Our enquirer may find this dispiriting. It seemed important to try to define the word, as a way of getting clear about what to believe, but if no one can answer the question 'What is humanism?' with a clear definition, then how are you to know whether or not to call yourself a humanist? And if it's such an ill-defined term, should we perhaps scrap it altogether and use other words instead to label our beliefs?

Here it is worth noting that the search for definitions has always been a philosophical minefield. The ancient Greek philosopher Plato, writing in the fourth century BCE, regularly portrayed his hero Socrates asking people for definitions, and reducing them to confusion in their attempts to provide them. In particular Socrates sought for definitions of important value terms: 'What is *goodness*?', 'What is *beauty*?', 'What is *justice*?' In one of his works Plato describes Socrates in conversation with two famous Athenian generals who have a great reputation for courage, asking them what courage is, and showing that they can't answer.[i] Every attempted definition which they come up with either excludes cases which they would want to call examples of courage, or lets in cases which wouldn't properly be called 'courage' at all, and so every attempt leads to absurd and unacceptable conclusions. Eventually they give up and allow Socrates to persuade them that though they're supposed to be models of courage they don't really have any idea what courage is.

But there is a different and more encouraging lesson we can draw from this. Socrates' demand for a definition took the form of a search for what we can call 'necessary and sufficient conditions'. A necessary condition for being 'courageous' is what we could also think of as a pre-requisite – it's something that you must have in order to count as 'courageous', that is to say, all people who are courageous will possess that quality. A sufficient condition for being 'courageous' is what we can think of as a guarantee – anyone who has this quality is bound to be courageous, that is to say, all people who possess that quality will be courageous. So if we can list the necessary and sufficient conditions of courage, it looks as though we'll have a fool-proof test of whether someone is courageous or not. The generals can't come up with such a list, and Socrates concludes that they don't really know what courage is. But that doesn't follow, for of course in a perfectly good sense they still know what courage is. They know how to use the word, and in particular they can give examples of things we would call 'courage'. As one of them says at the beginning of the discussion, courage is things like remaining at your post and not running away when danger threatens. Socrates is scornful of this. I don't just want an example, he says, I want to know what's common to all the examples which we call cases of courage. But the generals should have stood their ground. Giving examples, they should have said, is one perfectly good way of helping someone to see what 'courage' means. That is in fact the way that most of us come to learn the meaning of most words in our language, by encountering them in use and discovering the sorts of examples to which they are applied, rather than by learning abstract definitions.

We can tackle the question 'What is humanism?' in that spirit. We may not be able to come up with a simple list of necessary and sufficient conditions for being a humanist, but we can look at the sorts of beliefs which people who call themselves 'humanists' typically hold, and the sorts of beliefs which they typically reject, and we can also look at the sorts of beliefs which humanists themselves are likely to disagree about, and consider why they do so. In that way we can perhaps begin to get a clearer picture of what it is that people understand by 'humanism', focusing especially on how the word has been used within the humanist movement of which the British Humanist Association is a part. Having done so, we can then come back to the question of definition, and consider in what senses 'humanism' can and cannot be defined.

The rejection of religion

We begin with some brief historical points, if only in order to avoid confusion. The earliest use of the word 'humanist' refers to a branch of the educational curriculum. The Italian word 'umanista' was coined, probably in the late fifteenth or early sixteenth century, to denote a scholar or teacher of the *humanities* – the disciplines of grammar, rhetoric, poetry, history and moral philosophy.[ii] These studies were referred to by the Latin label *studia humanitatis*, a phrase which probably goes back to the fourteenth century and which implies a contrast between the study of 'humanity' and the study of divinity, of natural philosophy, and of vocational disciplines such as law and medicine. The humanists of the fourteenth to the sixteenth centuries, in Italy and in other European countries, were in particular interested in the study of the classical literature of ancient Greece and Rome, finding in it an ideal of human life which they wished to revive. By extension, later writers on the Italian Renaissance, from the nineteenth century onwards, have used the phrase 'Renaissance Humanism' to refer to that positive affirmation of the value of human life and human potentialities to be found in the art and literature of fifteenth century Italy – in the painting of Masaccio and the sculpture of Donatello, for instance, with its new interest in the celebration of the human form and the expression of human emotions. It is a view of life epitomised in the title of Pico della Mirandola's *Oration on the Dignity of Man*. 'Humanism' in this sense is consistent with, and was indeed incorporated into, a Christian religious framework, though involving a new emphasis on the importance of human free choice and the value of human achievements in this life rather than viewing this world as simply a preparation for the life to come. 'Humanism' in this sense is different from, though it has continuities with, the sense of the word with which we are concerned. Our interest is in humanism not just as an affirmation of human values and human potentialities, but as *an alternative to religious belief*. The word 'humanism' was first used in this sense in the nineteenth century, but the movement of thought to which it refers is much older than that. It can be traced back to some of the ancient Greek thinkers, and became an increasingly important current in the philosophical thought of the seventeenth and eighteenth centuries. It is with humanism in this sense that we shall be concerned in the rest of this discussion.

That gives us a starting point, then. Humanism, in the sense that we are interested in, is a view of the world which rejects religious beliefs. We could now get into a whole new search for a definition of 'religion', but we shall simply say that humanists do not believe in the existence of a god or gods. By 'gods' we mean beings who, like human beings, possess the attributes of intellect and will, have beliefs and knowledge and can make choices and decisions to act, but who are immensely more knowledgeable and more powerful than human beings, and whose supernatural power lies behind some or all of the natural forces we see at work in the universe. *Theists* typically believe that many or perhaps all of the things that happen in the world are ultimately to be explained as the results of the actions of a god or gods. Humanists, in contrast, are either atheists or agnostics. *Atheists* simply believe that there are no gods. *Agnostics* say that they do not know whether there is a god — or perhaps, more strongly, that we *cannot* know whether such beings exist - and that we must therefore get on with our lives without relying on any such religious belief.

It is worth emphasising that atheists do not, any more than agnostics, need to claim that they can *prove* that there is *not* a god. They need only claim that there are no sufficiently good reasons for believing that there is a god, and that in the absence of such reasons, we should not hold such a belief. Consider, for instance, the traditional 'argument from design' for the existence of a god. The argument is that the existence of innumerable species of plants and animals, all with physical organs and patterns of behaviour which make them intricately adapted to survival in their particular environment, is evidence that the world was created by a divine designer. Humanists are likely to say that the Darwinian theory of evolution provides a better explanation. New species have come about, over vast periods of time, as a result of accumulated random genetic mutations, and existing species are adapted to their environment because they are the products of those mutations which provide better adaptation and have therefore survived and reproduced themselves.

This doesn't mean that 'Darwin has refuted religious belief'. The existence of a divine creator is a *possible* explanation of adaptation and the appearance of design, but the Darwinian theory is a *better* explanation. It is better because it is more economical, and does not appeal to mysterious and inexplicable processes, but can be backed up with detailed explanations of the mechanisms of genetic mutation, genetic inheritance, and the struggle for survival. So the argument from design, which might have been a reason for believing in a god, turns out to be not a very good reason when contrasted with the alternative explanation. We can't look here at all the possible reasons which people might give for believing in a god, but humanists would say that it is up to religious believers to come up with good reasons, that they haven't succeeded in doing so, and that that's why we should be atheists or agnostics.

This commitment to rational argument – to the requirement that beliefs should be based on good reasons – is a very important feature of humanism, and we'll come back to it later. Humanists would say that it's not good enough to support religious beliefs by saying that their truth has been revealed by inspired priests or prophets. To say 'The truths of religion must be true because they have been revealed to us by God' is all too obviously circular. Again, it's not good enough to say something like

'I just feel that somehow there must be a god', or 'My faith comforts me and gives me an assurance that God cares for me', for such feelings are indistinguishable from wishful thinking. They are not genuine *reasons*. The commitment to reason is why humanists reject not only traditional religious beliefs but also all superstitions.

That then is the negative side of humanism, but the word also implies a positive side: that a belief in human beings can, in some sense, serve as an alternative to religious belief. What can this mean? This is where things start to get more complicated and where we have to accept that there is no humanist orthodoxy. We have no alternative but to try to tackle for ourselves the question: in what sense, if any, should we affirm a positive belief in humanity or in human beings?

Someone who rejected religious belief might see this as grounds for nothing other than despair. They might conclude that, in the absence of any divinely ordained purpose, human life is meaningless. There is, they might feel, nothing worth living for, and since all human endeavours lead only to death they are tainted with futility. Alternatively they might feel that though there are in principle things that can make human life worthwhile, human beings are incapable of achieving them unless they are guided and restrained by religious belief. They might, for instance, take the view that human beings are selfish and competitive and that only moral rules which are thought to be the commands of an all-powerful god can prevent us from destroying one another. An atheist who took this pessimistic view of human life might conclude that, though religious beliefs are false and illusory, it would be better if their falsity was not proclaimed and the illusion was sustained.

For humanists, by contrast, the rejection of religious belief can be given a more optimistic interpretation – but what kind of optimism, and why should we call it 'humanist'? What is it about human life and human beings that can provide grounds for optimism? Consider one version of humanist optimism, the version sometimes referred to as 'the Enlightenment Project'. The phrase refers to the sorts of beliefs associated with the philosophers and thinkers of the eighteenth century Enlightenment. Here are some typical Enlightenment beliefs and assumptions:

- Religious creeds serve the vested interests of the priesthood and of secular rulers.
- Once the superstitions of religious belief have been removed from people's minds, human life can be guided by a universally shared reason.
- Reason in the form of science can give us knowledge of the natural world and enable us to control it so as to promote human progress.
- Reason can also give us a scientific understanding of the way in which human behaviour is shaped by the social environment, and this knowledge can likewise be used to change the social environment so as to shape human beings in the right way and there by promote human progress.
- Good human lives consist in the enjoyment of happiness and pleasure and the prevention of pain and suffering, and such lives can be achieved by the employment of reason.
- Because human beings share a common human nature, the happiness and well-being of individuals can be made to coincide with the happiness and well-being of society.

This set of beliefs cannot straightforwardly be attributed to any one of the Enlightenment philosophers, but they are representative of many of the thinkers of that era, and some such package has often been associated with humanism since then.[iii] The Enlightenment Project has had a bad press in recent years, so it might help us to get clearer about the character of humanist optimism if we consider how far humanists should be committed to the Enlightenment Project, how much of it can be defended and how much of it should be rejected.

Optimism about progress

An optimistic belief in human progress has become difficult to sustain in the light of recent history. The decline of religious belief and the growing secularisation at least of European societies has not ushered in the rule of enlightened reason. Though religion still lies at the root of many conflicts, terrible things have, over the past century, been done in the name of secular ideologies and values. They have included the Nazi concentration camps and extermination programmes, the Stalinist labour camps, the area bombing of cities by both sides in the Second World War, the dropping of the atomic bombs on Hiroshima and Nagasaki, and carpet bombing and indiscriminate massacre in Vietnam. These acts have been motivated by a variety of non-religious beliefs and values, both noble and ignoble – nationalism, fascism, nazism, communism, freedom and democracy.

These experiences of the last hundred years have been enough to destroy a naïve belief in human progress, but it may be said that the problem goes deeper than that, and that humanism itself bears some responsibility for this catalogue of disasters and atrocities. They are, it might first be said, examples of what happens when the restraints of religion, or of moral rules backed by a supernatural authority, are removed. The attitude expressed in the famous words of a character in Dostoevsky's novel *The Brothers Karamazov* – 'If God does not exist, then everything is permitted' – may once have looked like a promise of liberation, but can perhaps now be seen as a warning of nightmares to come. Secondly it might be said, in criticism of humanism, that the historical record has been a lesson in what follows from the idealisation of humanity. Faith in human nature turns out to be misguided, critics may say, now that we know the terrible deeds which can be committed not only by tyrants and psychopaths but by ordinary human beings, people like you or me, just doing their job or obeying orders or following the crowd. Trust in human reason, it may be said, turns out to be a misplaced trust in nothing more substantial than a capacity to design ever more efficient instruments of destruction. Finally, the pursuit of an ideal of 'humanity' can be criticised as making it all too easy to label whole classes of human beings (Jews, for instance, or blacks, or the disabled, or homosexuals) as 'not fully human' and thus to embrace racist and other programmes of discrimination or even extermination.

What lessons should humanists learn from this? We will turn in the next section to the question of a humanist morality, and the possibility of values without religion. What about the dangers in the idealisation of humanity? Humanists need not and should not assume that the removal of religious superstition is the only thing needed for human goodness to be liberated and for rationality to prevail. Some strands of the humanist tradition did, in the nineteenth century, take the form of attempts to establish a new religion, 'the religion of humanity', but we can now see that for the folly that it was. A credible contemporary humanism must distance itself from any such idealisation of human powers and potentialities.

Humanists do not have to accept any naïve belief in the essential goodness of human nature. We know that in certain circumstances ordinary human beings can do terrible things. By the same token, however, we also know that some human beings, in some circumstances, are capable of the most extraordinary acts of heroism and courage and love. Side by side with the catalogue of atrocities we could set a list of the people who opposed these evils, sometimes at the cost of their own lives. Humanists can therefore acknowledge the darker side of human nature without having to revert to a secular version of the Christian idea of 'original sin'. It makes little sense to talk of human nature either as 'essentially good' or as 'essentially evil'. Human beings are what they are, a complex mixture. We know that whatever is best in human beings can be perverted and corrupted and destroyed, as a consequence of other equally deep-rooted features of human life, weaknesses and irrationalities which we can seek to understand and inhibit but which we cannot ignore. There is no guarantee that the human capacity for good must triumph, but also no reason to suppose that it must fail.

Likewise a reliance on human reason need not be equated with a naïve trust that rationality will prevail. Any sober and realistic assessment of the prospects for the improvement of the human condition has to acknowledge that much of human behaviour is driven by deeply irrational forces, and that religion is only one manifestation of these. To say that human beings are rational is not to claim that they will always think and act rationally, but that they have the capacity to do so, and that they should seek to exercise that capacity. To those who say 'Reason is an unreliable guide, forget your reason and trust your instincts', the answer must be 'Which instincts?' It is all very well to say 'Trust your instinctive feelings of pity and sympathy for your fellow human beings.' It is quite another thing to urge people to surrender themselves to 'gut feelings', or to let themselves be caught up in mass hysteria or the excitement of the moment, or to follow blindly the will of the leader who claims to be instinctively in tune with the will of the people. Those are precisely the kinds of irrationality which underlie so many of the crimes of the past century, and our powers of rational thought and judgement are our only defence against such dangers. The appeal to reason doesn't mean divesting ourselves of spontaneous feelings and emotions. It does mean making rational judgements about which feelings are to be trusted and which are not.

In distancing our humanism from the idealisation of humanity, from a naïve belief in human progress or from a naïve faith in human nature and human rationality, we can perhaps draw on a useful distinction made by the French philosopher Jean-Paul Sartre, in his influential 1945 lecture 'Existentialism is a Humanism', between two kinds of optimism and two corresponding kinds of humanism:

> In reality, the word humanism has two very different meanings. One may understand by humanism a theory which upholds man as the end-in-itself and as the supreme value. Humanism in this sense appears, for instance, in Cocteau's story *Round the World in 80 Hours*, in which one of the characters declares, because he is flying over mountains in an aeroplane, "Man is magnificent!"... That kind of humanism is absurd, for only the dog or the horse would be in a position to pronounce a general judgment upon man and declare that he is magnificent, which they have never been such fools as to do – at least, not as far as I know.[iv]

To this Sartre contrasts his 'existentialist' humanism, which consists not in any belief in the inevitability of human progress or the essential goodness of man, but in the belief that whether human life will get better or worse, and whether 'man' will turn out to be good or bad, depends on the free choices of individual human beings. 'Man is nothing else but that which he makes of himself'.[v]

Optimism about values

We have suggested that humanism should distance itself from the over-optimistic belief in human progress which is one element in what we have referred to as the Enlightenment Project. We turn now to another characteristic feature of Enlightenment thinking, the claim that human reason can, without the aid of divine revelation, establish the values and moral principles which should guide human actions. There are some very complex issues here, which give rise to deep philosophical disagreements, and which we need to disentangle. In particular we must try to distinguish those views which are characteristically humanist and those on which humanists can sensibly disagree with one another.

Consider the claim that human beings are the source of all value. There's a sense in which this is a claim which humanists ought to accept, but the sense needs to be properly defined. Most obviously, it stands in contrast to the counter-claim made by many religious believers, that only if we have a set of moral rules revealed to us by a divine authority can we know how we ought to live. This is one of the most resilient features of religious belief, expressed in the vocabulary of 'commandments' and 'obedience', 'sin' and 'forgiveness'. Many (though by no means all) religious believers talk as though they have a monopoly on moral understanding. Humanists will of course reject the appeal to divine authority, not only because they reject the belief in a god but also because they think that such an appeal is unnecessary. A central feature of any decent morality will be a recognition that we should take account of one another's needs and interests.

Humanists can see that what enables human beings to live this way is not a feeling of awe or reverence for divine authority or a fear of divine retribution, but the ties of love and affection, loyalty and fellow-feeling, attitudes of respect and concern, and the networks of social relationships which are deep-rooted features of human life. The appeal to evolutionary theory can help here, not as an alternative appeal to authority but as confirmation of the obvious fact that humans have evolved as a social species, equipped with the psychological capacities which they need for cooperation. Again there are no guarantees of sweetness and light, but also no need for despair.

There is another position which can be contrasted with the humanist one. There is a philosophical tradition which attributes to 'values' an independent existence separate from the natural world and from human life. The classic formulation is that of Plato, who argued that values and other abstract ideas exist as a reality outside space and time and outside the world of sensory experience. This committed him to the view that even if human beings (or any other conscious beings) did not exist there would still be such things as goodness and justice. Though such a position may not be logically incompatible with some kind of humanism, it is unlikely that humanists would endorse it. It is more plausible to maintain that talk of 'value', of 'right' and 'wrong', 'good' and 'bad', reflects our understanding of what matters to us as human beings, from a human perspective, in the light of human needs and interests. It is in that sense that we might say that human beings are the source of value.

This still leaves us with a lot of difficult philosophical questions about values, and any definition of humanism ought to leave them as open questions. We have commented negatively on a kind of 'Platonic realism', but there remains a philosophical debate between what are called 'realist' and 'anti-realist' views about values. The 'realists' would say that though values do not exist in some sort of Platonic heaven, the facts that certain actions are right or wrong, cruel or kind, just or unjust, are real moral facts. 'Anti-realists' would maintain that there is an important distinction to be made between 'facts' and 'values', and that whereas facts about the world are there to be discovered, values are things we choose or create or invent, or project onto the world as a reflection of our feelings and desires. No resolution of this debate is in sight, and any attempt to resolve it must depend on precise and complex analyses of terms such as 'fact' and 'value', 'belief' and 'desire' and the like.

There is no humanist orthodoxy on these difficult questions. Nevertheless we think that just as humanism should distance itself from a 'divine command' theory of morality or a Platonic realism, so also it should distance itself from what we shall call 'crude subjectivism' and 'crude relativism'. ('Crude' is a loaded term, but the positions we have in mind *are* crude.) The crude subjectivist says: 'It's up to you what you think about right and wrong, everybody else's opinion is just their opinion and no one has the right to disagree with you.' What the crude relativist says is very similar but perhaps expressed in more collective terms: 'What you think about right and wrong is just your point of view, it's just a reflection of your background and the culture you happen to have been brought up in.' The relativist version is likely to be backed up by assertions such as that 'we're all conditioned by society'.

What these often-encountered positions rule out is the possibility of *rational argument*. Value-judgements are not just blind instincts and urges, they can and should be backed up by reasons, and the giving of reasons is a necessary condition of both agreement and meaningful disagreement. If people disagree about, say, the rights and wrongs of abortion, or war, or social inequalities, their differences are not like the difference between those who do and those who don't like the taste of roast parsnips. The parties to a moral dispute don't just differ, they *disagree*, and that means that they think their opponents are missing something, are mistaken in some way, and can be given reasons to think differently. This commitment to rational argument is, we have already said, integral to humanism. It includes a commitment to rational argument about *moral* questions, and it is part of what needs to be retained from the Enlightenment Project. There is no guarantee that the giving of reasons will lead to eventual agreement. Nevertheless the activity of reason-giving is by its nature a search for agreement. To give you reasons for a moral position which I hold is to invite you to see it as a position which you too could and should hold. Moreover there are some grounds for optimism about the possibility of moral agreement, and those grounds are provided by our shared human nature. Human beings may differ in their tastes, their liking or disliking of parsnips, but they share basic needs, not only biological needs for food and drink, shelter and good health, but also psychological needs for love and affection, for recognition and support, for independence and interdependence. As social beings we also have a capacity to sympathise with others' feelings of enjoyment and suffering, and some predisposition to find ourselves in harmony with other people's emotions and attitudes. Our common humanity makes it at least possible for us to share a common vocabulary of values and to give and to recognise shared reasons for moral conclusions.

Talk of 'human nature' and a 'common humanity' has been viewed with suspicion by some philosophers. The suspicion has sometimes been formulated in the language of a recent philosophical tendency which has been called 'postmodernism' and which sometimes opposes itself to what it calls 'humanism'. These critics point out that the appeal to a common humanity can mask real differences of class and gender and race, and that the imposition of supposedly shared human values can amount to a kind of intellectual and moral imperialism which silences other voices and excludes other experiences. That is a real danger, and it should alert us against too quick and too easy an appeal to 'human nature', but it need not require us to abandon the idea. There *has* been slow but real progress towards sexual equality and racial equality over the centuries, and that progress has taken the form not only of recognition of differences but, more importantly, of greater recognition of what human beings have in common, undermining glib sexist talk of 'separate spheres' and racist talk of 'inferior breeds'.

We should therefore resist the arguments of those who preach the total failure of the Enlightenment Project. Such philosophers are inclined to assert that there is no universal set of rational ethical standards, but only separate and distinct moral traditions, each with its own internal standards and internal values. The values of different moral traditions are said to be 'incommensurable', that is, they cannot be compared and weighed against one another in order to arrive at a judgement which takes these different kinds of values into account. Experience suggests otherwise. Moral debate between people from radically different starting points does not always end in sterile deadlock. People from different traditions can come to understand one another's position, and can do so because different moral traditions are all attempts to make sense of the same shared human condition, a world in which human beings are born and die, love and hate, procreate and grow old, fight and cooperate. Humanists should not give up on rational argument, and to that extent they should remain committed to at least a part of the Enlightenment Project. To repeat, there is no guarantee of ultimate moral convergence, and there may in the end turn out to be radical differences of moral perspectives and values which cannot be resolved, but the only way we can find out is by committing ourselves to at least the search for agreement through reasoned debate.

Which values?

We have asserted the possibility of shared human values. It is time that we said something about what those values might be. One suggestion may readily occur at this point: that if human beings are the *source* of value, then the only thing that can *have* value must be the satisfaction of human desires, that is, human happiness and the prevention of human suffering. However, that conclusion doesn't follow, and though there is some truth in it, it's too simple.

Its attraction is the attraction of *Utilitarianism*, the moral theory associated especially with the philosophers Jeremy Bentham in the late eighteenth century and John Stuart Mill in the mid-nineteenth century.[vi] Theirs was one of the most influential and important attempts to establish a moral theory on purely secular foundations. The theory asserts what they called 'the greatest happiness principle': that actions are right to the extent that they promote pleasure and happiness and prevent pain and suffering, and wrong to the extent that they produce suffering and prevent happiness. Utilitarianism has an obvious appeal and many humanists have endorsed it as the best candidate for a rational secular approach to moral questions.

We should note immediately that utilitarianism doesn't just assert the value of *human* happiness. As Bentham rightly emphasised, if pleasurable experiences have value and painful experiences have disvalue, then it follows that we owe moral concern to *any* being which is capable of experiencing pleasure and pain – in other words, any *sentient* being. Consistent utilitarians will therefore recognise that they ought to be concerned to promote animal welfare and prevent animal suffering. Humanists, if they are utilitarians, don't have to maintain that human interests are the only things that are morally important.

In any case we should question the assumption that humanists have to be utilitarians. This is another matter on which there is deep philosophical disagreement, and which our definition of humanism should leave as an open question. Consider for instance the moral theory of Immanuel Kant, a contemporary of Bentham, whose ethics is often seen as a principal alternative to utilitarianism.[vii] Kant recognises moral duties to promote the well-being of others, but he also recognises duties even more fundamental, to respect other human beings as rational agents in their own right, with their own purposes and projects. He speaks of the recognition of human dignity, which requires us not to use other human beings simply as objects, as means for our own ends, however elevated those ends may be. Kant is one source for the modern emphasis on human *rights*, for instance the rights of human beings not to be killed or enslaved or exploited.

Utilitarians, it might seem, are committed to accepting that it may be morally permissible to kill innocent human beings, if by so doing we can produce for others enough happiness to outweigh the loss of happiness and the suffering of the killed and the bereaved. Kantians might say that, however admirable it may be to try to promote human happiness, certain ways of doing so are morally ruled out, and that includes the deliberate killing of the innocent. It is a matter for philosophical debate which way the argument should go here. Sophisticated utilitarians will argue that a sufficiently complex and subtle version of utilitarianism can accommodate the insights of Kantian ethics. Our definition of humanism will need to allow for either position, but certainly at a practical level a plausible humanist morality has to find room for the importance of ideas of human dignity, human freedom and autonomy, and human rights.

The worries about utilitarianism which we have mentioned are worries about its emphasis on judging actions by their *consequences*. Utilitarians seem to be committed to the kind of position encapsulated in the phrase 'the end justifies the means'. That is to say, it seems that they have to accept that absolutely *any* kind of action – punishing the innocent, torturing people, enslaving people, killing the innocent, even mass murder – could in principle be morally permitted if, in particular circumstances, it produced enough good to outweigh the harm. Utilitarians may counter that such circumstances will never arise in practice, but critics will say that the problem goes deeper than that. Kant offers one diagnosis of what the utilitarian might be missing, but there are other ways of expressing the worries about utilitarianism. Another way of putting it might be to say that utilitarianism focuses too exclusively on the *consequences* of actions and not enough on the nature of *the actions themselves* - whether they are just or unjust, honest or dishonest, kind or cruel, considerate or inconsiderate, and so on. This is not to say that it is never under circumstances acceptable to do anything which is dishonest, or unjust, but it is to say that the qualities of justice, honesty, kindness and the like are important because they are the kinds of qualities which make someone *a good human being*. To talk in this way is to use the language of what have traditionally been called 'the virtues'. It is a way of thinking about morality which goes back to Plato and Aristotle, and is still a live option in moral philosophy.[viii] It is one which might be attractive to humanists, because it locates values in an account of the nature of human beings and of what it is to be a good human being. Utilitarians can reply that we still need an account of why the virtues are *good* qualities for a human being to possess, and can argue that they are in fact good qualities only because acting on them will make for greater happiness overall. So we see again the resilience of utilitarianism as a plausible theory, but also the kinds of criticisms which it would have to deal with.

As a final comment on the possible limitations of utilitarianism, we should also leave open the possibility that humanists might ascribe value to things quite distinct from human life or human experiences or the experiences of other sentient beings. Take the case of concern for the environment. There are obvious reasons for such concern which make reference to human interests. We want to have unspoilt countryside to enjoy, we want to be able to appreciate the peace and tranquillity of remote places, we want clean air to breathe and unpolluted water to drink or to bathe in, and we also want to preserve the habitats of other animals. Over and above all this, however, some environmentalists would say that beautiful landscapes and unspoilt wildernesses have *intrinsic* value, a value in their own right, quite apart from their *instrumental* value as means to human enjoyment and well-being. Humanists may debate the rationality of such a position, but it's another matter on which our definition of humanism should remain neutral.

So, though considerations of what will promote human well-being and help to reduce human suffering will have an important and central place in any humanist morality, they need not be the whole of it. How far and in what ways it will extend beyond those central concerns will be a proper matter for rational debate among humanists. What that commitment to rational debate *will* exclude, we suggest, is a morality consisting entirely of simple and dogmatic general rules – a 'ten commandments' morality. Rules may have a place in a humanist morality, perhaps as useful rough-and-ready guides for conduct, perhaps as something stronger than that, but humanists will not accept a simple list of rules either as revealed moral wisdom or as self-evident truths. 'Thou shalt not commit adultery'? Humanists will want to dig deeper, to ask about the nature of love and its relation to exclusivity, and to think about what exactly is involved in the values of loyalty and fidelity. 'Thou shalt not steal'? Humanists will want to look more closely at the importance of private property, and its relation to other aspects of social and economic justice. 'Thou shalt not bear false witness'?

Humanists will recognise the importance of honesty and trust as features of our relations with one another, but will also want to ask whether that rules out the possibility of ever telling a lie for the sake of some greater good.

There are also traditional moral rules which have been widely accepted in the past but which rest on nothing other than an appeal to religious authority, and which humanists will simply reject. Typical examples are rules prohibiting certain kinds of sexual practices, such as homosexuality or masturbation. Some fundamentalist Christians try to support such rules by quoting from the scriptures, but a sentence from the Bible or from any other religious text is not by itself a rational basis for any moral position. The deepest feature of the humanist approach to morality, then, is the commitment to the importance of rational thought and debate.

Optimism in the face of human mortality

We referred earlier to the attitude of despair which some see as the outcome of a loss of religious belief. This can include the idea that if life on this earth is the only life there is, and leads only to the grave, then no human achievements, transitory as they are, can have any value. Some religious believers will claim that only the promise of immortality can give our lives a meaning and a purpose. Humanists reject that false promise. They believe that this life is the only life we have. The conscious experiences that make up our lives are tied to the existence of a physical body, including a brain and nervous system, and when the body ceases to function, those conscious experiences cease too. Humanism embraces an acceptance of the inevitability of our own deaths and the deaths of those we love, without any false sentimentality or phony consolations. Hence the practical importance (and growing popularity) of humanist funeral ceremonies, which allow for the frank acknowledgement of grief and loss, without the need to 'look for the resurrection of the dead, and the life of the world to come.'[ix]

Humanist funeral ceremonies do not just serve for the expression of grief.

They are also the celebration of a life. That is a kind of optimism, but an optimism that is authentic and hard-won. It is a recognition that the pleasures and achievements of that life were real and have not been undone by death; that even a life which has included its share of pain and tragedy has been a unique and irreplaceable human endeavour; and that those who live on can find their lives enriched by the memory of the person who has died. It is also an opportunity to recognise that we in turn may be remembered after our deaths, that how we live now can help to shape the future after we are gone, and that those continuities can give our lives a significance which transcends our individual life-span. This is not to postulate any mystical idea of a collective self, a greater 'spirit' of which we are all a part. There are, in an important sense, only individual lives, but their meaning is given to them in part by those who have gone before and by those who will come after.

Once again there are no guarantees. In some cases of grief and loss there may simply be no consolation. It may be, for instance, that the sudden death of a child whose life seemed full of promise cannot be seen as anything other than a tragic and pointless waste, and humanists reject the false consolation of a faith that all is really for the best as part of some inscrutable divine plan. But humanists also refuse the global conclusion that the inevitability of death renders *all* human activity pointless.
If someone has lived a long and happy and useful life and has achieved things which have also contributed to the lives of others, then they have not lived in vain. There is tragedy in human existence, but there is also fulfilment. Any philosophy of life has to give a sense to the great inescapable facts of the human condition, of birth and procreation and death. Humanism tries to do so.

The problem of definition revisited

We have discussed both the negative and the positive side of humanism. The negative side is the rejection of religious belief. The positive side is the belief that in virtue of our capacities as human beings we can live good and meaningful lives without the false consolations of religion. We have distinguished that positive side from a naively optimistic belief in the inevitability of human progress. We have associated it with the recognition that human beings can make choices and by doing so can shape their own future for better or for worse. We have associated it with the belief that human beings are the source of value, and can through rational debate and argument attempt to agree on shared values and a shared morality. We have recognised that our definition of humanism should leave open some fundamental questions about what those values should be and about what their logical status is. Finally we have suggested that humanism incorporates an acceptance of the fact of human mortality and the possibility of finding something positive in the continuity of human life despite the experience of grief and loss.

In what sense, then, have we provided a definition? We have not given a set of necessary and sufficient conditions, such that any view of the world which satisfies those conditions, and only one which does so, must be called 'humanism'. But it is true of a great deal of our language, even of many of the ordinary words we use in everyday discourse, that they cannot be defined by specifying necessary and sufficient conditions. We think we know what a 'chair' is. We might even attempt a definition: 'A chair is a piece of furniture for sitting on.' But is a bean-bag a chair? Is a futon a chair? They have some features in common with what we normally call 'chairs' but other features are different. In this way most of our concepts have what has been called 'open texture'. Their boundaries cannot be sharply demarcated.

A helpful view of the problem of definition can be found in the work of the twentieth-century philosopher Ludwig Wittgenstein. He suggests that often, when we are looking for an account of the meaning of a word, it is a mistake to suppose that there must be something common to all applications of the word. Rather, there are what he calls 'family resemblances' between different uses of the word. He takes the example of the word 'game'. Is there something common to all the things we call 'games'?

Don't just assume that there must be, says Wittgenstein, look and see. Often games are activities engaged in for fun, but what about modern professional sports? Often games involve competition, and winning and losing, but what about patience, or throwing a ball against a wall and catching it? If we are looking for why all these things are called 'games', what we shall find is not some common essence, some one feature or set of features which they all possess, but 'a complicated network of similarities overlapping and criss-crossing'. Wittgenstein says: 'I can think of no better expression to characterize these similarities than "family resemblances"; for the various resemblances between members of a family: build, features, colour of eyes, gait, temperament, etc. etc. overlap and criss-cross in the same way.'[x]

The 'family resemblances' account is particularly applicable to the word 'game' because the concept of a game is something that has changed and developed over time. The same is true of the uses of the word 'humanism'. There are thin strands connecting Renaissance Humanism with modern humanism. There are thicker strands connecting eighteenth- and nineteenth-century versions of humanism with humanism as we have characterised it, but we have emphasised also the ways in which we think that the concept has had to change. If we had to provide a descriptive account encompassing everything to which the word 'humanism' can be applied, or even all the facets of modern humanism, the account would be pretty thin and lacking in content. We would do better to trace the continuities and discontinuities.

Another useful notion which can help us to get clear about the problem of definition is that of 'essentially contested concepts'. Examples are moral and political concepts such as 'freedom' or 'justice' or 'democracy'. Attempts to define such concepts have to recognise that there is no single understanding of them, but rather, different and competing interpretations of what they consist in, and our attempts at definitions will seek to capture what it is that we think is valuable about such things. So, for instance, a socialist and an advocate of a market society will give different accounts of what they think genuine 'justice' is. A conservative and a radical will want to offer competing definitions of 'democracy'. 'Humanism' can likewise be seen as an essentially contested concept. There are competing versions of it, competing interpretations of how it should be understood. If we were to try to characterise what is common to all these competing interpretations, our comprehensive account would have very little content. The account which we have offered here has, we might say, been not *descriptive* but *prescriptive*. We have tried to say what we think humanism *ought* to be. We have offered what we take to be a defensible and plausible interpretation of humanism, whilst recognising also that our account must be broad enough to leave many questions of interpretation as open to disagreement.

If someone were to insist that we summarise our account in the form of a definition, perhaps the best that we could offer would be something like this: Humanism is an evolving tradition of thought which starts from the rejection of religious belief and attempts, through rational argument and debate, to work out the positive implications of that starting point.

If you accept that starting point and want to be involved in that on-going debate, you are probably a humanist.

Footnotes

i The discussion comes in Plato's *Laches*.

ii Augusto Campana, 'The Origin of the Word "Humanist"', in *Journal of the Warburg and Courtauld Institutes*, Vol.IX (1946); Paul Oskar Kristeller, *Renaissance Thought: the Classic, Scholastic and Humanist Strains* (New York, 1961); Kristeller, 'Humanism', in *The Cambridge History of Renaissance Philosophy*, ed. Charles B Schmitt and Quentin Skinner (Cambridge, 1988). The earliest use of the word 'humaniste' in French is in 1552 (see Campana p.70), and the Oxford Dictionary gives the earliest occurrence of the English word 'humanist', used in this same sense, as 1589. An exhaustive survey of the history of the different uses of the word 'humanism' can be found in Nicholas Walter, *Humanism: What's in the Word* (Rationalist Press Association, London, 1997).

iii Perhaps the Enlightenment philosopher who comes closest to exemplifying them is Baron d'Holbach, in his *Système de la nature* of 1770.

iv Jean-Paul Sartre, *Existentialism and Humanism*, trans. Philip Mairet (Methuen, London, 1948), pp.54-5.

v Ibid. p.28. In the lecture Sartre goes on to assert that in choosing for myself I choose for all human beings, and that in assessing my choices I should therefore always ask myself 'What if everyone did that?' This suggestion seems to owe more to the moral philosophy of Kant than to Sartre's brand of existentialism. To say as he does 'In fashioning myself I fashion man' (p.30) appears to be at odds with his emphasis on the *individual* character of choice and decision. It was perhaps in part for this reason that Sartre subsequently disowned the lecture and regretted that it had been published.

vi Mill's essay *Utilitarianism* was first published in 1861. Some modern editions (for instance the one edited by Mary Warnock, published by Fontana, London, 1962) also include extracts from Bentham's writings, such as his *Introduction to the Principles of Morals and Legislation*, first published in 1789.

vii Kant's classic presentation of his moral theory is his *Groundwork of the Metaphysics of Morals* (the title is sometimes also translated as *Fundamental Principles of the Metaphysics of Morals*), first published in 1785.

viii This is a strand in Plato distinct from his talk of values as existing in some supersensible realm. It is what could fairly be called the more humanist strand in Plato. His pupil Aristotle (384-322 BCE) rejected Plato's theory of supersensible values but shared his 'virtue ethics'.

ix It's worth noting that in any case the promise of immortality, even if it were credible, would not itself serve to confer meaning on human existence. If someone finds their life pointless, they would be unlikely to find it any less pointless if they discovered that it would last for ever. Indeed, the prospect of a life continuing endlessly into the future might come to seem unbearably repetitive and tedious. The prospect is dramatized in the play *The Makropulos Case* by Karel Čapek, which was made into an opera by Janaček and is discussed by the philosopher Bernard Williams in a paper 'The Makropulos case: reflections on the tedium of immortality' (in Bernard Williams, *Problems of the Self*, Cambridge University Press, Cambridge, 1973).

x Ludwig Wittgenstein, *Philosophical Investigations* (Basil Blackwell, Oxford, 1953), paragraphs 66-67.

Humanist Philosophers' Group

Those wanting to know more about the British Humanist Association and the Humanist Philosophers' Group can do so by looking at the BHA website: www.humanism.org.uk

or contacting the BHA at
47 Theobalds Road
London WC1X 8SP
Tel: 020 7430 0908.

Students who would like to know more about how humanists apply their worldview to practical ethical issues will find briefings on the following on www.humanism.org.uk:

Abortion
Animal Welfare
Crime and Punishment
Discrimination and Prejudice
Drugs
Embryo Research
Environmental Issues
Euthanasia
Family Matters
Genetic Engineering
Human Rights
Immigration and Asylum
Sexuality and STDs
Suffering and evil
Suicide
War
World Poverty